50 Classic French Desserts

By: Kelly Johnson

Table of Contents

- Crème Brûlée
- Tarte Tatin
- Macarons
- Clafoutis
- Madeleines
- Profiteroles
- Eclairs
- Soufflé au Chocolat
- Mille-Feuille
- Paris-Brest
- Mousse au Chocolat
- Galette des Rois
- Financiers
- Choux à la Crème
- Canelés
- Tarte aux Fruits
- Croustillant au Chocolat
- Charlotte aux Fraises
- Tarte au Citron Meringuée
- Pain de Gênes
- Pâté de Pâques
- Gâteau Basque
- Flognarde
- Tarte Bourdaloue
- Biscuit de Savoie
- Kouign-Amann
- Crêpes Suzette
- Vacherin
- Poached Pears in Red Wine
- Gâteau Opéra
- Croustade
- Charlotte Royale
- Far Breton
- Quatre-Quarts
- Bûche de Noël

- Tarte au Chocolat
- Pithiviers
- Tarte à la Rhubarbe
- Gâteau de Mamie
- Croissant aux Amandes
- Macaron au Pistache
- Gâteau Saint-Honoré
- Chaussons aux Pommes
- Crème Caramel
- Savarin
- Nougat
- Pain Perdu
- Chiboust
- Flan Parisien
- Merveilles

Crème Brûlée

Ingredients:

- 2 cups heavy cream
- 1 vanilla bean (or 1 tablespoon vanilla extract)
- 5 large egg yolks
- 1/2 cup granulated sugar
- 2 tablespoons light brown sugar (for topping)

Instructions:

1. Preheat the oven to 325°F (160°C). Place 4 ramekins in a baking dish.
2. In a saucepan, heat the heavy cream and vanilla bean (split and scraped) over medium heat until just boiling. Remove from heat and let it steep for 5 minutes. If using vanilla extract, add it later.
3. In a mixing bowl, whisk together the egg yolks and granulated sugar until smooth.
4. Gradually add the warm cream to the egg mixture, whisking constantly to prevent curdling.
5. Strain the mixture through a fine sieve into a clean bowl, discarding the vanilla pod.
6. Pour the custard into the ramekins, filling them almost to the top.
7. Carefully pour hot water into the baking dish around the ramekins, ensuring the water comes halfway up the sides.
8. Bake for 40-45 minutes until the custard is just set but still slightly wobbly in the center.
9. Remove from the oven and cool completely. Refrigerate for at least 2 hours or overnight.
10. Just before serving, sprinkle a thin layer of light brown sugar over each custard and caramelize with a kitchen torch until golden and crisp.

Tarte Tatin

Ingredients:

- 6-8 medium apples (such as Braeburn or Granny Smith)
- 1/2 cup unsalted butter
- 1/2 cup granulated sugar
- 1 teaspoon vanilla extract
- 1 sheet puff pastry (or shortcrust pastry)
- Pinch of salt

Instructions:

1. Preheat the oven to 375°F (190°C).
2. Peel, core, and quarter the apples. Set aside.
3. In a 9-inch oven-safe skillet, melt butter over medium heat. Add sugar and cook, swirling the pan occasionally, until the mixture turns golden brown and begins to caramelize.
4. Carefully arrange the apple quarters in the caramel, packing them tightly. Cook for 10 minutes until the apples begin to soften.
5. Remove the skillet from heat and stir in vanilla extract and a pinch of salt.
6. Roll out the puff pastry and drape it over the apples, tucking the edges into the pan.
7. Bake for 25-30 minutes, or until the pastry is golden brown and puffed.
8. Let it cool for 5 minutes, then invert the tart onto a serving plate. Serve warm.

Macarons

Ingredients:

- 1 3/4 cups powdered sugar
- 1 cup almond flour
- 3 large egg whites
- 1/4 cup granulated sugar
- 1/2 teaspoon vanilla extract
- Food coloring (optional)
- Filling of choice (ganache, buttercream, or jam)

Instructions:

1. Preheat the oven to 300°F (150°C). Line a baking sheet with parchment paper.
2. Sift together the powdered sugar and almond flour into a bowl.
3. In a separate bowl, whisk the egg whites until soft peaks form. Gradually add the granulated sugar, continuing to whisk until stiff peaks form.
4. Fold the almond flour mixture into the egg whites until smooth and glossy. Add food coloring if desired.
5. Transfer the batter to a piping bag and pipe small circles (about 1-inch diameter) onto the prepared baking sheet.
6. Tap the baking sheet on the counter to release air bubbles and let the macarons rest for 30 minutes to form a skin.
7. Bake for 15-18 minutes, allowing the macarons to form a slight "foot" at the bottom.
8. Let the macarons cool completely before removing them from the parchment paper.
9. Pipe your chosen filling onto one macaron shell and sandwich with another shell.

Clafoutis

Ingredients:

- 1 1/2 cups whole milk
- 3 large eggs
- 1/2 cup granulated sugar
- 1 teaspoon vanilla extract
- 1/2 cup all-purpose flour
- 1/4 teaspoon salt
- 1 1/2 cups pitted cherries (or other fruit)
- Powdered sugar (for dusting)

Instructions:

1. Preheat the oven to 375°F (190°C). Butter a 9-inch pie dish or tart pan.
2. In a mixing bowl, whisk together the milk, eggs, sugar, vanilla extract, flour, and salt until smooth.
3. Pour the batter into the prepared dish.
4. Arrange the cherries evenly in the batter.
5. Bake for 35-40 minutes until puffed and golden.
6. Let cool slightly and dust with powdered sugar before serving.

Madeleines

Ingredients:

- 1 cup all-purpose flour
- 1/2 teaspoon baking powder
- 1/4 teaspoon salt
- 1/2 cup unsalted butter, melted
- 2/3 cup granulated sugar
- 2 large eggs
- 1 teaspoon vanilla extract
- Zest of 1 lemon

Instructions:

1. Preheat the oven to 375°F (190°C). Grease and flour a Madeleine pan.
2. In a small bowl, whisk together the flour, baking powder, and salt.
3. In a separate bowl, whisk together the sugar and eggs until light and fluffy. Add the melted butter, vanilla extract, and lemon zest, mixing until smooth.
4. Fold in the dry ingredients until just combined.
5. Spoon the batter into the Madeleine pan, filling each mold about 2/3 full.
6. Bake for 10-12 minutes until golden brown.
7. Let the Madeleines cool slightly before removing from the pan. Serve warm or at room temperature.

Profiteroles

Ingredients:

- 1 cup water
- 1/2 cup unsalted butter
- 1 cup all-purpose flour
- 4 large eggs
- 1/2 teaspoon vanilla extract
- 1 cup heavy cream (for filling)
- 1/4 cup powdered sugar (for filling)
- Chocolate sauce or ganache (for topping)

Instructions:

1. Preheat the oven to 425°F (220°C) and line a baking sheet with parchment paper.
2. In a saucepan, bring water and butter to a boil. Add flour and stir until the dough pulls away from the sides of the pan.
3. Remove from heat and let cool for 5 minutes. Add eggs one at a time, stirring until smooth.
4. Spoon or pipe the dough into small mounds on the baking sheet.
5. Bake for 20-25 minutes, until golden and puffed. Let cool.
6. Whip the heavy cream with powdered sugar until soft peaks form. Cut the profiteroles in half and fill with whipped cream.
7. Drizzle with chocolate sauce or ganache and serve.

Eclairs

Ingredients:

- 1 cup water
- 1/2 cup unsalted butter
- 1 cup all-purpose flour
- 4 large eggs
- 1/2 teaspoon vanilla extract
- 1 cup heavy cream
- 1/4 cup powdered sugar
- 1/2 cup chocolate (for glazing)

Instructions:

1. Preheat the oven to 425°F (220°C). Line a baking sheet with parchment paper.
2. In a saucepan, combine water and butter and bring to a boil. Stir in flour and cook until the dough pulls away from the sides.
3. Remove from heat, then add eggs one at a time, stirring well after each addition.
4. Pipe the dough onto the prepared baking sheet in 4-inch long strips.
5. Bake for 20-25 minutes until golden. Cool.
6. Whip heavy cream with powdered sugar until stiff peaks form.
7. Cut the eclairs in half and fill with whipped cream.
8. Melt chocolate and drizzle over the eclairs before serving.

Soufflé au Chocolat

Ingredients:

- 4 ounces dark chocolate
- 3 tablespoons unsalted butter
- 3/4 cup milk
- 1/4 cup granulated sugar
- 3 large eggs, separated
- 1/2 teaspoon vanilla extract
- Pinch of salt
- Powdered sugar (for dusting)

Instructions:

1. Preheat the oven to 375°F (190°C). Butter and sugar two ramekins.
2. Melt the chocolate and butter together in a saucepan over low heat. Stir in the milk and sugar until smooth.
3. Remove from heat and whisk in egg yolks and vanilla extract.
4. In a separate bowl, whisk the egg whites and salt until stiff peaks form.
5. Gently fold the egg whites into the chocolate mixture.
6. Pour the batter into the prepared ramekins and bake for 12-15 minutes, until puffed and set.
7. Dust with powdered sugar and serve immediately.

Mille-Feuille

Ingredients:

- 1 sheet puff pastry
- 1 cup vanilla custard (or pastry cream)
- Powdered sugar (for dusting)

Instructions:

1. Preheat the oven to 400°F (200°C). Roll out the puff pastry and cut into 3 equal strips.
2. Bake the pastry strips for 12-15 minutes until golden and crispy.
3. Once cooled, layer custard between the pastry sheets.
4. Dust the top with powdered sugar and serve.

Paris-Brest

Ingredients:

- 1 cup water
- 1/2 cup unsalted butter
- 1 cup all-purpose flour
- 4 large eggs
- 1/4 teaspoon salt
- 1/2 teaspoon vanilla extract
- 1 cup hazelnut cream (or praline paste)
- Powdered sugar (for dusting)

Instructions:

1. Preheat the oven to 400°F (200°C). Line a baking sheet with parchment paper.
2. In a saucepan, combine water, butter, and salt. Bring to a boil.
3. Add the flour all at once, stirring vigorously until the dough forms a ball.
4. Remove from heat and let cool for 5 minutes. Add eggs one at a time, mixing until smooth after each addition.
5. Pipe the dough into a ring shape on the prepared baking sheet. Bake for 25-30 minutes until golden and puffed.
6. Let the ring cool completely.
7. Slice the Paris-Brest in half and fill with hazelnut cream.
8. Dust with powdered sugar and serve.

Mousse au Chocolat

Ingredients:

- 8 ounces dark chocolate (70% cocoa)
- 3 tablespoons unsalted butter
- 1/4 cup strong coffee (optional)
- 3 large eggs, separated
- 1/2 cup heavy cream
- 2 tablespoons sugar

Instructions:

1. Melt the chocolate and butter together in a heatproof bowl over simmering water or in the microwave. Stir until smooth. Add coffee if using.
2. Let the chocolate mixture cool slightly, then whisk in the egg yolks.
3. Whisk the egg whites until stiff peaks form and fold them gently into the chocolate mixture.
4. In a separate bowl, whip the cream and sugar until soft peaks form.
5. Fold the whipped cream into the chocolate mixture until smooth.
6. Spoon the mousse into individual cups and chill in the fridge for at least 2 hours.
7. Serve chilled, optionally garnished with whipped cream or chocolate shavings.

Galette des Rois

Ingredients:

- 2 sheets puff pastry
- 1/2 cup almond flour
- 1/4 cup powdered sugar
- 1/4 cup unsalted butter, softened
- 1 egg
- 1 teaspoon vanilla extract
- 1 tablespoon dark rum (optional)
- 1 egg (for egg wash)

Instructions:

1. Preheat the oven to 375°F (190°C). Line a baking sheet with parchment paper.
2. Roll out one sheet of puff pastry on the prepared baking sheet.
3. In a bowl, combine almond flour, powdered sugar, butter, egg, vanilla, and rum (if using). Mix until smooth.
4. Spread the almond filling over the center of the pastry, leaving a border around the edges.
5. Place a fève (a small ceramic figurine) or a dried bean in the filling if desired.
6. Cover with the second sheet of puff pastry and press the edges to seal.
7. Brush the top with a beaten egg for a golden finish.
8. Bake for 25-30 minutes, or until golden and puffed.
9. Let cool slightly before serving.

Financiers

Ingredients:

- 1/2 cup unsalted butter
- 1/2 cup almond flour
- 1/4 cup all-purpose flour
- 1/2 cup powdered sugar
- 1/4 teaspoon salt
- 4 large egg whites
- 1 teaspoon vanilla extract

Instructions:

1. Preheat the oven to 375°F (190°C). Grease a financier mold or mini muffin tin.
2. Melt the butter in a saucepan until it turns golden brown (beurre noisette).
3. In a bowl, sift together the almond flour, all-purpose flour, powdered sugar, and salt.
4. Whisk the egg whites until soft peaks form.
5. Fold the dry ingredients into the egg whites, then add the melted butter and vanilla extract.
6. Spoon the batter into the molds, filling each about 3/4 full.
7. Bake for 10-12 minutes, or until golden brown.
8. Let cool before serving.

Choux à la Crème

Ingredients:

- 1 cup water
- 1/2 cup unsalted butter
- 1 cup all-purpose flour
- 4 large eggs
- 1/4 teaspoon salt
- 1 cup heavy cream
- 2 tablespoons powdered sugar
- 1 teaspoon vanilla extract

Instructions:

1. Preheat the oven to 400°F (200°C). Line a baking sheet with parchment paper.
2. In a saucepan, combine water, butter, and salt. Bring to a boil.
3. Add the flour all at once and stir until the dough forms a ball.
4. Remove from heat and let cool for 5 minutes. Add eggs one at a time, mixing until smooth after each addition.
5. Pipe small mounds of dough onto the baking sheet and bake for 25-30 minutes until puffed and golden.
6. Whip the heavy cream with powdered sugar and vanilla until soft peaks form.
7. Once the choux are cool, slice them in half and fill with whipped cream.
8. Serve immediately or chill until ready to serve.

Canelés

Ingredients:

- 1 cup whole milk
- 1/2 cup granulated sugar
- 1/4 cup unsalted butter
- 1 vanilla bean
- 1 tablespoon rum
- 1/2 cup all-purpose flour
- 2 large eggs
- 1 egg yolk
- 1 tablespoon cornstarch

Instructions:

1. Preheat the oven to 375°F (190°C). Grease canelé molds with butter.
2. In a saucepan, heat milk, sugar, butter, and the vanilla bean (split and scraped) over medium heat until it just begins to boil.
3. Remove from heat and let cool slightly. Add rum.
4. In a separate bowl, whisk together flour, eggs, egg yolk, and cornstarch.
5. Gradually add the milk mixture to the egg mixture, whisking until smooth.
6. Let the batter rest in the fridge for at least 2 hours.
7. Pour the batter into the molds, filling each about 3/4 full.
8. Bake for 45-60 minutes, or until dark golden brown.
9. Allow to cool slightly before removing from the molds.

Tarte aux Fruits

Ingredients:

- 1 sheet shortcrust pastry
- 1 cup pastry cream (or custard)
- Assorted fresh fruits (berries, kiwi, peaches, etc.)
- Apricot glaze (or fruit jelly)

Instructions:

1. Preheat the oven to 375°F (190°C). Roll out the pastry and line a tart pan.
2. Bake the pastry shell for 15-20 minutes until golden brown. Let cool completely.
3. Fill the cooled tart shell with pastry cream.
4. Arrange the fresh fruit on top of the cream in a decorative pattern.
5. Brush the fruit with apricot glaze to give it a shiny finish.
6. Chill the tart for 1 hour before serving.

Croustillant au Chocolat

Ingredients:

- 1/2 cup dark chocolate (70% cocoa)
- 1/2 cup milk chocolate
- 1/4 cup hazelnuts, toasted and chopped
- 1/4 cup crushed cookies (biscuit or digestive)
- 1/4 cup puffed rice or rice crisps

Instructions:

1. Melt both chocolates together in a heatproof bowl over simmering water or in the microwave.
2. Once melted, stir in the toasted hazelnuts, crushed cookies, and puffed rice.
3. Pour the mixture into a mold or a parchment-lined pan.
4. Chill in the fridge for 2 hours until firm.
5. Slice into pieces and serve.

Charlotte aux Fraises

Ingredients:

- 1 1/2 pounds fresh strawberries
- 1/2 cup sugar
- 1/2 cup water
- 2 tablespoons gelatin
- 1 cup heavy cream
- 1/4 cup powdered sugar
- 1 package ladyfingers
- 1 tablespoon cognac or fruit liqueur (optional)

Instructions:

1. Puree the strawberries with sugar in a blender. Strain through a sieve to remove seeds.
2. Dissolve gelatin in the water and heat until melted. Stir into the strawberry puree.
3. Whip the heavy cream with powdered sugar until stiff peaks form.
4. Fold the whipped cream into the strawberry mixture until smooth.
5. Line a mold with ladyfingers, creating a ring along the sides. Pour the strawberry mousse into the center.
6. Chill for 4 hours or overnight until set.
7. Remove from the mold, garnish with fresh strawberries, and serve chilled.

Tarte au Citron Meringuée (Lemon Meringue Tart)

Ingredients:

- **For the tart crust:**
    - 1 1/4 cups all-purpose flour
    - 1/4 cup powdered sugar
    - 1/2 teaspoon salt
    - 1/2 cup unsalted butter, cold and cubed
    - 1 egg yolk
    - 2-3 tablespoons ice water
- **For the lemon filling:**
    - 1 cup lemon juice (about 4-5 lemons)
    - 1 tablespoon lemon zest
    - 3/4 cup sugar
    - 4 large eggs
    - 1/4 cup unsalted butter, cubed
    - 1/4 cup cornstarch
- **For the meringue:**
    - 4 large egg whites
    - 1/2 cup sugar
    - 1/4 teaspoon cream of tartar
    - 1 teaspoon vanilla extract

Instructions:

1. **Make the tart crust:** Preheat the oven to 350°F (175°C). In a food processor, combine flour, powdered sugar, and salt. Add butter and pulse until the mixture resembles coarse crumbs. Add egg yolk and water, pulsing until dough comes together. Press dough into a tart pan and chill for 30 minutes. Bake for 20-25 minutes or until golden brown. Set aside to cool.
2. **Make the lemon filling:** In a saucepan, combine lemon juice, zest, sugar, and cornstarch. Heat over medium heat, whisking until thickened. Remove from heat and whisk in the eggs and butter until smooth. Pour into the cooled tart shell.
3. **Make the meringue:** Whip the egg whites with cream of tartar until soft peaks form. Gradually add sugar and vanilla, whipping until stiff peaks form. Spread meringue over the lemon filling, making decorative peaks.
4. **Bake:** Bake at 350°F (175°C) for 10-15 minutes until the meringue is golden. Let cool before serving.

Pain de Gênes

Ingredients:

- 1/2 cup unsalted butter, softened
- 3/4 cup sugar
- 3 large eggs
- 1 cup almond flour
- 1/2 cup all-purpose flour
- 1/4 teaspoon baking powder
- 1/4 teaspoon salt
- 1/4 cup rum or kirsch
- Powdered sugar (for dusting)

Instructions:

1. Preheat the oven to 350°F (175°C). Grease and flour a loaf pan.
2. Beat the butter and sugar until light and fluffy. Add eggs one at a time, beating well after each addition.
3. In a separate bowl, combine almond flour, all-purpose flour, baking powder, and salt. Gradually add this to the butter mixture, alternating with the rum or kirsch.
4. Pour the batter into the prepared pan and bake for 45-50 minutes, or until a toothpick comes out clean.
5. Let cool before removing from the pan. Dust with powdered sugar before serving.

Pâté de Pâques

Ingredients:

- 2 sheets puff pastry
- 1/2 pound ground pork
- 1/2 cup cooked rice
- 1/4 cup cooked onions
- 2 hard-boiled eggs, chopped
- 1/4 teaspoon salt
- 1/4 teaspoon black pepper
- 1 egg (for egg wash)

Instructions:

1. Preheat the oven to 375°F (190°C). Roll out one sheet of puff pastry and place it on a baking sheet.
2. Mix the ground pork, rice, onions, chopped eggs, salt, and pepper in a bowl.
3. Spread the pork mixture in the center of the pastry, shaping it into a log.
4. Cover with the second sheet of puff pastry and seal the edges. Brush with the beaten egg for a golden finish.
5. Bake for 40-45 minutes, or until golden brown. Let rest for 10 minutes before slicing.

Gâteau Basque

Ingredients:

- **For the dough:**
    - 1 1/2 cups all-purpose flour
    - 1/2 cup sugar
    - 1/4 teaspoon salt
    - 1/2 cup unsalted butter, softened
    - 1 egg
    - 1 teaspoon vanilla extract
    - 1 tablespoon rum (optional)
- **For the filling:**
    - 1/2 cup pastry cream
    - 1/4 cup cherry jam (or any fruit jam of choice)

Instructions:

1. Preheat the oven to 375°F (190°C). Grease a round tart pan.
2. To make the dough, combine flour, sugar, and salt. Add butter, egg, vanilla, and rum. Mix until a smooth dough forms.
3. Roll out two-thirds of the dough and line the tart pan. Fill with pastry cream and a thin layer of jam. Roll out the remaining dough and place it on top, sealing the edges.
4. Bake for 30-35 minutes until golden brown. Let cool before serving.

Flognarde

Ingredients:

- 2 cups fruit (cherries, plums, apples, or berries)
- 3 large eggs
- 3/4 cup milk
- 1/2 cup sugar
- 1/2 cup all-purpose flour
- 1/4 teaspoon salt
- 1 teaspoon vanilla extract

Instructions:

1. Preheat the oven to 375°F (190°C). Grease a tart pan or baking dish.
2. Arrange the fruit in a single layer in the prepared pan.
3. In a bowl, whisk together eggs, milk, sugar, flour, salt, and vanilla until smooth.
4. Pour the batter over the fruit and bake for 30-40 minutes, or until puffed and golden.
5. Let cool before serving, optionally dusted with powdered sugar.

Tarte Bourdaloue

Ingredients:

- 1 sheet shortcrust pastry
- 1 can pears (or fresh pears)
- 1/2 cup almond cream (frangipane)
- 1/4 cup sliced almonds
- 1 tablespoon apricot jam (optional)

Instructions:

1. Preheat the oven to 375°F (190°C). Line a tart pan with the shortcrust pastry.
2. Drain the pears and slice them thinly. Arrange them in a circular pattern in the tart shell.
3. Spread the almond cream over the pears and sprinkle with sliced almonds.
4. Bake for 25-30 minutes, until the almond cream is golden.
5. Optional: Heat apricot jam and brush it over the tart for a glossy finish.

Biscuit de Savoie

Ingredients:

- 6 large eggs, separated
- 1 cup sugar
- 1 cup all-purpose flour
- 1/4 teaspoon salt
- Powdered sugar (for dusting)

Instructions:

1. Preheat the oven to 350°F (175°C). Grease a round cake pan and dust with flour.
2. Whisk the egg yolks with sugar until pale and thick. In a separate bowl, sift the flour and salt.
3. Fold the flour mixture into the egg yolk mixture.
4. Whisk the egg whites until stiff peaks form and gently fold them into the batter.
5. Pour the batter into the prepared pan and bake for 20-25 minutes.
6. Let cool, then dust with powdered sugar before serving.

Kouign-Amann

Ingredients:

- 1 sheet puff pastry
- 1/2 cup sugar
- 1/4 cup unsalted butter, melted
- 1/2 teaspoon vanilla extract
- Pinch of salt

Instructions:

1. Preheat the oven to 400°F (200°C). Grease a muffin tin.
2. Roll out the puff pastry and cut into squares. Place a dollop of butter and sugar in the center of each square.
3. Fold the pastry into a ball and place it in the muffin tin. Repeat with the remaining squares.
4. Bake for 20-25 minutes, or until golden brown and puffed.

Crêpes Suzette

Ingredients:

- **For the crêpes:**
    - 1 cup all-purpose flour
    - 1/2 cup milk
    - 1/2 cup water
    - 2 large eggs
    - 1/4 teaspoon salt
    - 2 tablespoons butter, melted
- **For the sauce:**
    - 1/2 cup unsalted butter
    - 1/4 cup orange juice
    - 1/4 cup orange liqueur (Grand Marnier or Cointreau)
    - 1/4 cup sugar

Instructions:

1. To make the crêpes, whisk together the flour, milk, water, eggs, salt, and melted butter. Heat a non-stick skillet over medium heat and cook thin crêpes, flipping once. Set aside.
2. For the sauce, melt the butter in a skillet over medium heat. Add the orange juice, liqueur, and sugar. Stir until the sugar dissolves.
3. Fold the crêpes into quarters and place them in the sauce. Let them soak for 1-2 minutes on each side.
4. Flame the crêpes with the remaining liqueur and serve immediately.

Vacherin

Ingredients:

- **For the meringue:**
    - 6 large egg whites
    - 1 1/2 cups sugar
    - 1 teaspoon vanilla extract
    - 1/2 teaspoon lemon juice
- **For the filling:**
    - 2 cups whipped cream
    - 1/2 cup mixed berries (such as raspberries, strawberries, and blueberries)

Instructions:

1. Preheat the oven to 225°F (110°C). Line two baking sheets with parchment paper.
2. Whisk the egg whites until soft peaks form. Gradually add sugar, vanilla extract, and lemon juice. Continue whipping until stiff peaks form.
3. Spoon the meringue onto the prepared baking sheets, forming two round discs. Bake for 1.5 to 2 hours, or until the meringues are crisp.
4. Once cooled, gently remove the meringues from the parchment paper and set one aside for the base and the other for the top.
5. Whip the cream until stiff and fold in the berries. Spread the whipped cream mixture over the meringue base and top with the second meringue.
6. Serve immediately or refrigerate for a few hours.

Poached Pears in Red Wine

Ingredients:

- 4 pears, peeled and cored
- 1 bottle red wine
- 1/2 cup sugar
- 1 cinnamon stick
- 1 star anise
- 1 vanilla bean, split and scraped
- Zest of 1 orange

Instructions:

1. In a large saucepan, combine the red wine, sugar, cinnamon stick, star anise, vanilla bean, and orange zest. Bring to a simmer.
2. Add the pears and cook gently for 30-40 minutes, or until tender. Turn the pears occasionally to ensure they cook evenly.
3. Once the pears are tender, remove them from the liquid and set aside.
4. Increase the heat to reduce the wine mixture by half, creating a syrup. Strain the syrup to remove the spices.
5. Serve the pears with the reduced syrup poured over them.

Gâteau Opéra

Ingredients:

- **For the almond sponge (Joconde):**
    - 1/2 cup almond flour
    - 1/2 cup powdered sugar
    - 1/4 cup all-purpose flour
    - 4 large eggs
    - 2 tablespoons butter, melted
- **For the coffee syrup:**
    - 1/2 cup strong coffee
    - 2 tablespoons sugar
    - 2 tablespoons coffee liqueur (optional)
- **For the chocolate ganache:**
    - 1 cup heavy cream
    - 8 ounces dark chocolate, chopped
- **For the buttercream:**
    - 1/2 cup butter, softened
    - 1/2 cup powdered sugar
    - 1/4 cup espresso, brewed and cooled
    - 2 tablespoons coffee liqueur (optional)

Instructions:

1. Preheat the oven to 375°F (190°C). Grease and line a baking pan.
2. For the sponge, beat the almond flour, powdered sugar, flour, and eggs together until smooth. Fold in the melted butter. Spread the batter evenly in the pan and bake for 8-10 minutes.
3. For the coffee syrup, combine the coffee, sugar, and coffee liqueur in a saucepan. Simmer until the sugar dissolves, then set aside to cool.
4. For the ganache, heat the cream until it begins to simmer, then pour over the chopped chocolate. Stir until smooth and glossy. Let it cool.
5. For the buttercream, beat the butter and powdered sugar until smooth. Add the cooled espresso and coffee liqueur, then mix until combined.
6. Assemble the cake by cutting the almond sponge into layers. Brush each layer with coffee syrup, then spread with a thin layer of buttercream. Repeat until all layers are stacked, finishing with a layer of ganache on top.
7. Let the cake set before serving.

Croustade

Ingredients:

- 1 sheet puff pastry
- 2 cups cooked apples, sliced
- 1/2 cup sugar
- 1/4 teaspoon cinnamon
- 1 tablespoon butter
- 1 egg (for egg wash)

Instructions:

1. Preheat the oven to 375°F (190°C). Roll out the puff pastry on a floured surface and fit it into a tart pan.
2. In a bowl, mix the cooked apples, sugar, and cinnamon.
3. Spread the apple mixture into the pastry shell and dot with butter.
4. Fold the edges of the pastry over the apples, leaving the center exposed. Brush with egg wash.
5. Bake for 30-40 minutes, or until the pastry is golden brown and the apples are tender.

Charlotte Royale

Ingredients:

- 1 prepared sponge cake, sliced into strips
- 2 cups whipped cream
- 1/2 cup raspberry puree
- 1/2 cup sugar
- 1 tablespoon gelatin (optional)

Instructions:

1. Line a round cake pan with plastic wrap. Arrange the sponge cake strips around the sides of the pan.
2. Whip the cream and mix with the raspberry puree and sugar. If using, dissolve the gelatin in a small amount of warm water and add to the cream mixture.
3. Pour the cream mixture into the center of the pan. Chill for several hours or overnight to set.
4. Unmold the cake and serve chilled.

Far Breton

Ingredients:

- 2 cups whole milk
- 1/2 cup sugar
- 3 large eggs
- 1 1/2 cups all-purpose flour
- 1/4 teaspoon salt
- 1 teaspoon vanilla extract
- 1 cup prunes (or raisins)

Instructions:

1. Preheat the oven to 350°F (175°C). Grease a baking dish.
2. In a bowl, whisk together the milk, sugar, eggs, flour, salt, and vanilla.
3. Add the prunes or raisins and stir to combine.
4. Pour the batter into the prepared dish and bake for 45-50 minutes, or until the top is golden and a toothpick comes out clean.
5. Let cool before serving.

Quatre-Quarts

Ingredients:

- 1 cup butter, softened
- 1 cup sugar
- 1 cup all-purpose flour
- 4 large eggs
- 1/4 teaspoon baking powder
- Pinch of salt

Instructions:

1. Preheat the oven to 350°F (175°C). Grease a loaf pan.
2. Cream the butter and sugar together until light and fluffy. Add the eggs one at a time, beating well after each addition.
3. Sift together the flour, baking powder, and salt, then fold into the butter mixture.
4. Pour the batter into the prepared pan and bake for 45-50 minutes, or until a toothpick comes out clean.

Bûche de Noël

Ingredients:

- **For the sponge cake:**
    - 4 large eggs
    - 1/2 cup sugar
    - 1/2 cup all-purpose flour
    - 1/4 teaspoon baking powder
    - 1/4 cup cocoa powder
- **For the filling:**
    - 1 cup heavy cream
    - 1/2 cup powdered sugar
    - 1 teaspoon vanilla extract
- **For the chocolate ganache:**
    - 1 cup dark chocolate
    - 1/2 cup heavy cream

Instructions:

1. Preheat the oven to 350°F (175°C). Grease a jelly roll pan.
2. For the sponge cake, beat the eggs and sugar until light and fluffy. Sift in the flour, baking powder, and cocoa powder, and fold gently.
3. Bake for 12-15 minutes until the sponge is firm. Let cool on a wire rack.
4. For the filling, whip the cream with the powdered sugar and vanilla until stiff peaks form.
5. For the ganache, heat the cream and pour it over the chocolate. Stir until smooth and let cool.
6. Once the sponge is cooled, spread the filling evenly and roll the cake into a log. Frost with ganache and decorate with chocolate shavings or powdered sugar.

Tarte au Chocolat

Ingredients:

- **For the crust:**
    - 1 1/4 cups all-purpose flour
    - 1/2 cup unsalted butter, cubed
    - 1/4 cup sugar
    - 1 egg yolk
- **For the filling:**
    - 8 ounces dark chocolate
    - 1 cup heavy cream
    - 1 tablespoon butter
    - 1/2 teaspoon vanilla extract

Instructions:

1. Preheat the oven to 350°F (175°C). Prepare a tart pan.
2. For the crust, combine the flour, butter, sugar, and egg yolk. Mix until dough forms. Press into the tart pan and bake for 10-12 minutes, or until golden.
3. For the filling, heat the cream and pour over the chopped chocolate. Stir until smooth. Add butter and vanilla.
4. Pour the chocolate filling into the cooled tart shell and refrigerate for at least 2 hours before serving.

Pithiviers

Ingredients:

- 2 sheets puff pastry
- 1 cup almond paste
- 1/2 cup sugar
- 2 tablespoons butter, softened
- 1 large egg (for egg wash)
- 1 tablespoon water

Instructions:

1. Preheat the oven to 375°F (190°C). Roll out one sheet of puff pastry and place it on a baking sheet lined with parchment paper.
2. Mix the almond paste, sugar, and butter together until smooth.
3. Spread the almond mixture onto the pastry, leaving a small border around the edges.
4. Place the second sheet of puff pastry over the almond mixture and press the edges to seal.
5. Using a knife, lightly score the top pastry in a decorative pattern. Brush with the egg wash (egg mixed with water).
6. Bake for 25-30 minutes, or until golden brown. Allow to cool before serving.

Tarte à la Rhubarbe

Ingredients:

- 1 sheet shortcrust pastry
- 2 cups rhubarb, chopped into 1-inch pieces
- 1/2 cup sugar
- 2 tablespoons cornstarch
- 1/2 teaspoon vanilla extract

Instructions:

1. Preheat the oven to 375°F (190°C). Line a tart pan with the shortcrust pastry and bake blind for 10 minutes.
2. In a bowl, toss the rhubarb with sugar, cornstarch, and vanilla extract.
3. Fill the tart shell with the rhubarb mixture and bake for 25-30 minutes, or until the rhubarb is tender and the crust is golden.
4. Let cool before serving.

Gâteau de Mamie

Ingredients:

- 1 cup butter, softened
- 1 cup sugar
- 3 large eggs
- 2 cups all-purpose flour
- 1 teaspoon baking powder
- 1/2 cup milk
- 1 teaspoon vanilla extract

Instructions:

1. Preheat the oven to 350°F (175°C). Grease and flour a cake pan.
2. Cream the butter and sugar together until light and fluffy. Add the eggs one at a time, mixing well after each addition.
3. Sift the flour and baking powder together, then add to the wet ingredients alternately with the milk. Stir in vanilla extract.
4. Pour the batter into the prepared pan and bake for 30-35 minutes, or until a toothpick inserted into the center comes out clean.
5. Allow to cool before serving.

Croissant aux Amandes

Ingredients:

- 6 croissants, cut in half horizontally
- 1/2 cup almond paste
- 1/4 cup sugar
- 1/4 cup butter, softened
- 1 egg
- Powdered sugar for dusting

Instructions:

1. Preheat the oven to 350°F (175°C).
2. Mix the almond paste, sugar, butter, and egg together to form a smooth almond filling.
3. Spread the almond filling inside each halved croissant.
4. Place the croissants on a baking sheet and bake for 10-12 minutes, or until golden brown and slightly puffed.
5. Dust with powdered sugar before serving.

Macaron au Pistache

Ingredients:

- **For the macaron shells:**
    - 1 cup powdered sugar
    - 1/2 cup almond meal
    - 3 large egg whites
    - 1/4 cup sugar
    - 1/4 teaspoon pistachio extract
- **For the pistachio filling:**
    - 1/2 cup unsalted butter, softened
    - 1/4 cup powdered sugar
    - 1/4 cup pistachio paste
    - 1/2 teaspoon vanilla extract

Instructions:

1. Preheat the oven to 300°F (150°C). Line a baking sheet with parchment paper.
2. For the macaron shells, sift together powdered sugar and almond meal. Whisk the egg whites until soft peaks form, then gradually add the sugar and continue whipping until stiff peaks form.
3. Gently fold in the almond mixture and pistachio extract. Pipe the batter onto the baking sheet in small circles.
4. Let the shells rest for 30 minutes before baking for 15-18 minutes, or until set.
5. For the filling, beat the butter, powdered sugar, pistachio paste, and vanilla together until smooth.
6. Once the shells are cool, pipe the pistachio filling onto one shell and sandwich with another. Let the macarons rest for a few hours before serving.

Gâteau Saint-Honoré

Ingredients:

- **For the pâte à choux (cream puff dough):**
    - 1/2 cup water
    - 1/4 cup butter
    - 1/2 cup all-purpose flour
    - 2 large eggs
- **For the puff pastry:**
    - 1 sheet puff pastry
- **For the caramel:**
    - 1 cup sugar
    - 2 tablespoons water
- **For the filling:**
    - 1 1/2 cups whipped cream
    - 1 tablespoon sugar

Instructions:

1. Preheat the oven to 400°F (200°C).
2. For the pâte à choux, combine water and butter in a saucepan. Bring to a boil, then add the flour and stir until a smooth dough forms. Remove from heat and stir in the eggs one at a time.
3. Pipe small puffs onto a baking sheet and bake for 15-20 minutes until golden.
4. Cut the puff pastry into a round and bake as per package instructions.
5. For the caramel, melt the sugar with water in a saucepan until golden brown.
6. Assemble the cake by filling the puff pastry with whipped cream. Dip the tops of the cream puffs into the caramel and arrange them around the edges of the puff pastry base.

Chaussons aux Pommes

Ingredients:

- 2 sheets puff pastry
- 4 apples, peeled, cored, and sliced
- 1/4 cup sugar
- 1 teaspoon cinnamon
- 1 tablespoon butter
- 1 egg (for egg wash)

Instructions:

1. Preheat the oven to 375°F (190°C).
2. In a saucepan, melt the butter and cook the apples, sugar, and cinnamon until softened.
3. Roll out the puff pastry and cut into squares. Spoon the apple mixture onto each square.
4. Fold the pastry over the filling to form a triangle. Seal the edges with a fork and brush with egg wash.
5. Bake for 20-25 minutes, or until golden brown.

Crème Caramel

Ingredients:

- 1/2 cup sugar (for caramel)
- 2 cups whole milk
- 1/2 cup sugar (for custard)
- 3 large eggs
- 1 teaspoon vanilla extract

Instructions:

1. Preheat the oven to 325°F (160°C).
2. For the caramel, melt 1/2 cup sugar in a saucepan over medium heat until golden. Pour the caramel into the bottom of individual ramekins and set aside.
3. For the custard, heat the milk and sugar until warm. In a separate bowl, whisk the eggs and vanilla extract. Gradually add the milk mixture to the eggs, stirring constantly.
4. Pour the custard into the caramel-lined ramekins and bake in a water bath for 45-50 minutes, or until set.
5. Let cool before serving.

Savarin

Ingredients:

- 2 1/4 cups all-purpose flour
- 1/4 cup sugar
- 1 teaspoon active dry yeast
- 1/2 cup warm milk
- 1/2 teaspoon salt
- 5 large eggs
- 1/2 cup unsalted butter, softened
- 1/4 cup rum (for soaking)
- 1/2 cup water (for soaking)
- 1/2 cup sugar (for syrup)
- Fresh fruit and whipped cream (for serving)

Instructions:

1. In a bowl, combine warm milk, yeast, and sugar. Let sit for 5 minutes until foamy.
2. Add flour, salt, and eggs. Mix until smooth. Let the dough rise for 1-2 hours in a warm place.
3. Once risen, knead in the butter until smooth. Place the dough into a well-greased savarin mold and let rise for another hour.
4. Preheat the oven to 350°F (175°C) and bake for 30-35 minutes until golden and cooked through.
5. For the syrup, combine sugar and water in a saucepan and bring to a boil. Remove from heat and stir in rum.
6. Once the savarin has cooled slightly, soak it in the syrup for about 5 minutes. Serve with fresh fruit and whipped cream.

Nougat

Ingredients:

- 2 cups honey
- 2 cups sugar
- 2 tablespoons water
- 3 large egg whites
- 1 1/2 cups toasted almonds
- 1 1/2 cups toasted pistachios
- 1/2 teaspoon vanilla extract
- A pinch of salt

Instructions:

1. In a saucepan, combine honey, sugar, and water. Bring to a boil and cook until the syrup reaches 245°F (118°C) on a candy thermometer.
2. While the syrup is cooking, beat the egg whites with a pinch of salt until stiff peaks form.
3. Gradually pour the hot syrup into the beaten egg whites while continuing to beat.
4. Stir in the vanilla extract and fold in the toasted almonds and pistachios.
5. Spread the mixture into a lined baking dish and let cool for several hours. Slice into squares and serve.

Pain Perdu (French Toast)

Ingredients:

- 4 slices of day-old bread (preferably brioche or challah)
- 1/2 cup whole milk
- 2 large eggs
- 1 tablespoon sugar
- 1/2 teaspoon cinnamon
- 1 teaspoon vanilla extract
- 2 tablespoons unsalted butter
- Powdered sugar and maple syrup for serving

Instructions:

1. In a bowl, whisk together the milk, eggs, sugar, cinnamon, and vanilla extract.
2. Heat butter in a skillet over medium heat.
3. Dip each slice of bread into the egg mixture, coating both sides, and cook in the skillet until golden brown on both sides.
4. Serve with powdered sugar and maple syrup.

Chiboust

Ingredients:

- 2 cups whole milk
- 1/2 cup sugar
- 1 vanilla bean or 1 tablespoon vanilla extract
- 3 large egg yolks
- 3 tablespoons cornstarch
- 1/2 cup heavy cream
- 3 large egg whites
- 1/4 cup sugar (for meringue)

Instructions:

1. In a saucepan, heat the milk and vanilla bean (or extract) until it begins to simmer.
2. In a separate bowl, whisk egg yolks, sugar, and cornstarch together. Slowly add the hot milk to the egg mixture, whisking constantly.
3. Return the mixture to the saucepan and cook over low heat, whisking constantly, until thickened.
4. In another bowl, beat the egg whites with sugar until stiff peaks form. Gently fold the meringue into the custard.
5. Whip the heavy cream until stiff and fold it into the mixture.
6. Serve as a filling for pastries or enjoy on its own.

Flan Parisien

Ingredients:

- 1 sheet shortcrust pastry
- 2 1/2 cups whole milk
- 1/2 cup sugar
- 1 teaspoon vanilla extract
- 4 large eggs
- 1 tablespoon cornstarch

Instructions:

1. Preheat the oven to 350°F (175°C) and line a tart pan with the shortcrust pastry. Bake for 10 minutes to set.
2. In a saucepan, heat the milk, sugar, and vanilla extract until simmering.
3. In a bowl, whisk the eggs and cornstarch. Gradually add the hot milk mixture, whisking constantly.
4. Pour the custard mixture into the tart shell and bake for 30-35 minutes until set and golden on top.
5. Allow to cool before serving.

Merveilles (French Fritters)

Ingredients:

- 2 cups all-purpose flour
- 1/4 cup sugar
- 1/2 teaspoon salt
- 3 large eggs
- 1/2 cup milk
- 1/2 teaspoon vanilla extract
- 2 cups vegetable oil (for frying)
- Powdered sugar for dusting

Instructions:

1. In a bowl, mix the flour, sugar, and salt together. Whisk in the eggs, milk, and vanilla extract to form a smooth batter.
2. Heat the vegetable oil in a large pot or deep fryer to 350°F (175°C).
3. Drop spoonfuls of batter into the hot oil and fry until golden brown and crispy, about 2-3 minutes.
4. Remove from the oil and drain on paper towels. Dust with powdered sugar and serve warm.